How an e-Book Works

by Amanda StJohn

Illustrated by Bob Ostrom

MEDIA ENHANCED BOOKS
AV²
BY WEIGL™
ADDED VALUE • AUDIO VISUAL

Go to **www.av2books.com**, and
enter this book's unique code.

BOOK CODE

H783969

AV² by Weigl brings you media enhanced
books that support active learning.

First published by

The Child's World

Published by AV² by Weigl
350 5ᵗʰ Avenue, 59ᵗʰ Floor New York, NY 10118
Website: www.av2books.com

Library of Congress Control Number: 2016956799

ISBN 978-1-4896-5965-1 (hardcover)
ISBN 978-1-4896-5966-8 (softcover)
ISBN 978-1-4896-5967-5 (multi-user eBook)

Printed in the United States in Brainerd, Minnesota
1 2 3 4 5 6 7 8 9 0 20 19 18 17 16

112016
110416

Text copyright ©2013 by Amanda StJohn
Illustrations copyright ©2013 by Bob Ostrom
Published in 2013 by The Child's World®

When Stew Rabbit arrived at the library, he marched to the children's room. He found his best friend and smiled. His bunny teeth shined. "Hey, Opal!"

"Hey," she called back.

Stew rubbed his cheek. "What are you doing there?"

"Reading this e-book," Opal Owl answered.

"What's an e-book?" Stew asked, sitting down.

"e-Book means electronic book," Opal explained. "Instead of reading words on the pages of a book, we read e-books on a computer or e-reader."

"And that's an e-reader?" asked Stew.

Opal held up her **device**. "Right. I read my e-books on this."

Opal handed Stew her e-reader. He peered at it and turned it around and upside down.

"My e-reader is a BookWorm," she added.

"There are other types of e-readers, then?" Stew was quite curious.

"Sure!" Opal whistled. "Just like there are different types of cars to drive around in, there are different kinds of e-readers to read e-books on."

"So," Stew began, "how does an e-book work?

Opal thought for a moment. "Well, how do you usually find library books?"

"Easy! I use the library **catalog**," said Stew.

"That's exactly what I did to find this e-book," agreed Opal.

Opal led Stew over to a computer station.

On her library's main Web site, she showed Stew the e-books catalog button. "Click this. You'll see e-books you can borrow from the library."

On the computer screen, Stew saw three lists. They said: "For Adults, For Teens, For Kids."

"Click 'For Kids?'" Stew guessed.

"Good job." Opal clicked on the list for kids. "Pick one, Stew. And if you don't see a book you like, you can always ask a librarian for help."

Stew found a book called *Sunny and Luna*. "That one!"

When Opal clicked on the *Sunny and Luna* book, the computer screen asked: "Which **format** do you want: PDF, EPUB, or BW?"

"What does this stuff mean?" asked Stew.

"Don't worry." Opal was cool as ever. "We want BW."

Stew raised his eyebrow. "How do you know?"

Opal answered, "BW stands for BookWorm. My e-reader takes BW formats. BookWorm's instructions told me."

Stew pointed at the other formats. "Other e-readers might read these formats?"

"Right," nodded Opal.

Opal clicked the correct format, then clicked "check out." Next, the computer screen asked for her library card number. Opal looked at her library card. She typed the number on her card into the computer. She double-checked her typing and clicked the OK button.

The computer went to a new Web site. Stew and Opal could see the cover of *Sunny and Luna*. The screen said, "Available to download."

"Can we read your e-book now?" asked Stew.

"Not yet," Opal shook her head no. "It's not on my e-reader yet."

"Well, how does an e-book get onto your e-reader?" pressed Stew.

"We **sync** up. Like this . . . " Opal opened her book bag. From a little pouch she pulled out a USB cord. Opal plugged one end of the cord into her BookWorm. She plugged the other end into the library computer.

"Press the BookWorm's power button," she said to Stew.

With the power on, the BookWorm connected to the computer.

"So what do we do next?" asked Stew.

"We follow the instructions on the screen," replied Opal. "If you have a different e-reader, the steps to download a book might be different. If you get stuck, a librarian can help you."

"So what do we have to do for your e-reader?" asked Stew.

"I'll show you," replied Opal. She pointed to the screen. "See the **icon** for my BookWorm? It appeared on the computer desktop when I plugged in my device."

She clicked on the *Sunny and Luna* link online and its icon appeared on the computer desktop, too. She dragged the book icon on top of the BookWorm icon. The computer screen said, "Download complete."

Stew smiled. "It's just like my MP3 player."

Next, they needed to eject their e-reader from the computer. This would end the sync and make sure the e-book was saved correctly. Opal clicked "Eject."

"You may now remove your device safely," the computer screen said.

Opal rolled up her USB cable. "I'd better put this away before I lose it."

She and Stew left the computer station so someone else could use it. They plopped onto a giant beanbag. On her BookWorm, Opal went to the main screen.

There, on the digital bookshelf, sat a copy of *Sunny and Luna*. Other e-books sat on Opal's bookshelf, too. She had *Wind in the Willows*, a story about a toad and a frog. There was even an e-book on how to bake cookies.

Opal's cookbook had a banner that said "2 days."

"What does that mean?" asked Stew.

"The cookbook is a library e-book," she explained.

"So, you have to return the book to the library in two days?" asked Stew.

"Kind of," Opal tilted her head. "Actually, you never have to return e-books."

Stew was puzzled. "Then . . . why does it say two days?"

"Because," began Opal, "in two days the e-book will disappear!"

"Nuh-uh. That's not true." Stew was sure Opal was teasing.

"It's totally true!" she squealed. "It goes poof!"

Stew thought about what happened when he returned a library book late. He had to pay money for a **fine**. "You don't have to pay any fines for e-books?"

"Never," declared Opal. "Because the book returns itself. Cool, huh?"

"How else is borrowing e-books different from borrowing books?" asked Stew.

"That sounds like a question for Ms. Mantis," said Opal.

Off they went to find Ms. Mantis, the children's librarian. Ms. Mantis was decorating the bulletin board with cutout clowns.

"Hi, Ms. Mantis," Stew said, clearing his throat.

Opal asked, "How is borrowing e-books different than borrowing books?"

"I like your question!" Ms. Mantis smiled. "Tell me, how many books can you take home at once?"

"Ten," answered Opal firmly.

"Well, you can have only two e-books at one time," said the librarian.

Learning this gave Stew a new thought. "Ms. Mantis?"

Stew stroked a whisker. "I return my books right after reading them. Can I return e-books early, too?"

"Sure," sang Ms. Mantis. "Plug in your BookWorm. I'll show you how."

Opal synced her device with the computer.

"See that little arrow by your book?"

Ms. Mantis paused. "Click it once."

The arrow showed some options. One said, "Return this book to the library."

"Wow," said Opal. "I didn't know about that."

Just to practice, Opal clicked the arrow by her cookbook. She clicked "Return this book" and the book disappeared—poof!

"Whoa," Stew gasped. "You weren't kidding, Opal! When a book goes poof!, it disappears for good!"

Key Words

catalog: the complete list of items a library has to offer; Stew and Opal searched the catalog for e-books to read

device: a piece of technology used for a specific purpose, like reading e-books; Opal used an e-reader device to read e-books

fine: money you pay if you damage, lose, or return a library book late; Stew will have to pay a fine is he doesn't return his library books on time

format: the way a digital file, such as an e-book, is saved on the computer; Opal's e-books were in the format used for BookWorm e-readers

icon: a picture image that represents an e-book, e-reader device, or other item on a computer; Opal saw the BookWorm icon on her computer desktop

sync: comes from the word synchronize, meaning to get two things to work together; Opal had to sync her e-reader with the library computer

Tips to Remember

- To check out library e-books, you need a library card.

- Don't share your library card with anyone.

- Use the advanced search feature to find only the e-books written in your e-reader's preferred format.

- Don't unplug your device until you eject it on the computer screen. This will make sure your files are saved correctly.

- Ask your librarian for help when you need it.

Check out www.av2books.com for activities, videos, audio clips, and more!

1 Go to www.av2books.com.

2 Enter book code. | H 7 8 3 9 6 9

3 Fuel your imagination online!